EGGS

—and what happens inside them

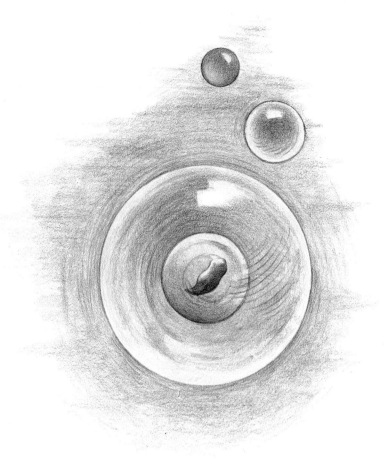

EGGS

—and what happens inside them

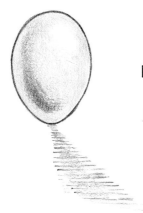

MARGARET COSGROVE

Illustrated by the author

DODD, MEAD & COMPANY
NEW YORK

To Peter Rabbit, Jr., and all the

Dependent Small Creatures

Contents

1. An Egg Is for What?

This could very well be a recipe book from its title. Do you prefer your eggs scrambled, poached or soft-boiled? With a little salt and pepper any kind is delicious. And eggs are so popping with food value that the hen has been turned into a factory, and her only product a huge industry. There is scarcely a farm or village in the world without its hens pecking about, producing eggs.

But this isn't a recipe book.

Of course most people have heard of Easter eggs, which, we are told, are laid by a celebrated rabbit named the Easter Bunny, whose eggs chicks hatch out of! How did such a notion ever begin? Perhaps (as some believe) a poor peasant mother once colored a

few eggs as an Easter surprise and hid them in the woods. Just as her children found them, a rabbit which chanced to be hiding nearby went hopping away, and the children believed that the rabbit had left them there. And so the story got around. Many a tale or bit of gossip has gotten its start in just such a way.

But this isn't a book about special holidays or old legends.

And then there are the very beautiful eggs given as gifts in many countries. The ancient Egyptians and Persians, many centuries ago, colored eggs and gave them as gifts during the spring festival. People of Czechoslovakia decorated eggs in the loveliest of designs, and in the Ukraine each village often has been known for its own particular design, painted with great skill and artistry. In Russia, jeweled eggs were once made, or carved from precious gems, and offered as gifts. In England friends wrote messages upon eggs and sent them to their friends.

But this isn't a book about beautiful art objects.

Eggs—they are more than Humpty Dumpty, or a fried egg sandwich, or gifts to be exchanged. But after all, a lot of this fits together to make sense. An egg seems the very symbol of life, just as spring does as it bursts forth after the long winter when all has seemed dead. Easter carries the message of new hope and eternal life; it tells us that death has been vanquished. An egg may be painted like the rays of the returning sun, the Northern Lights, flowers, birds, the stars, the joy of new birth. The rabbit—symbol of fertility and many babies—is born with its eyes open, "watching the sky." And the moon determines the date of Easter.

People have long had a feeling about the mystery of the egg. Some ancient peoples believed that the world hatched from a giant egg; others believed that the egg was a symbol of the moon. Nearly all life in some way springs from eggs, or an egg-like Idea. But what happens within the shell? How do new creatures get into eggs? How do they eat, breathe, grow, locked in their private world? And when can they come out—and how?

This is a book of how, what and when.

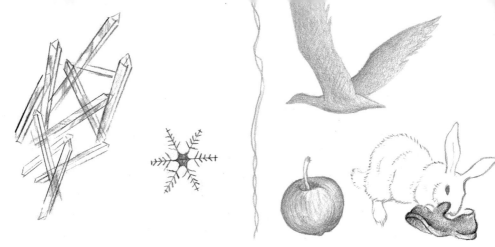

2. The Great Idea

The world is made up of living things and non-living things.

The non-living things, such as rocks and minerals, have their forms. Crystals of all shapes are the basic structures of many. But what of living things? There are so many kinds! Seaweed and bats and flowers and elephants; potatoes and snakes and toadstools and puppies; starfish, roots, eagles, skin and bones, bananas and grass....

They have to grow; rocks, in the same way, do not. To grow they have to take something into themselves from outside, make some of it into part of themselves, use up some for energy, and give off the rest, like ashes left after a fire, as waste products.

There was a time when there was no life on Earth. As life gradually developed in the waters, what form would it take? The Idea worked itself out over millions of years. For uncountable centuries all life was very tiny, and made of one cell, or unit. The Earth still contains much one-celled life, a great part of it in the waters: oceans, ponds, rivers, puddles. This kind, although it must be seen with a microscope (see p. 11), is very complicated inside—it isn't at all simple just because it's small! Each is a complete plant or animal form in itself. But it can never grow very large.

A CELL 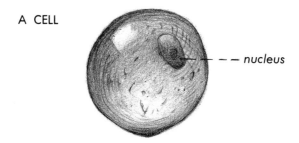 — — nucleus

But slowly the great Idea worked itself out farther, so that there were practically no limits to life—the size or kind, what it could do, what it would become. Creatures could grow to almost any size or variety, making the Earth rich with more kinds of life than the wildest imagination could ever dream up. The Idea meant that living things would no longer have to be of only one unit, or cell, but could be built of many cells—huge numbers of them, even thousands of millions. And in these big groupings of cells different ones would be doing different kinds of work instead of all the work having to be performed by tiny parts inside a single cell.

SOME ONE-CELLED LIFE

The great, basic Idea, then, is *the cell*—as the container for the processes of life, and as a basic building block that can be used with which to build and build.

A cell needs to make new cells, and it does it by growing, splitting in two in a certain way, and both new cells growing and dividing in two again, and so on. The new cells are usually the same kind as the one that divided. Single-celled animals usually make their own kind. In the body, the muscle cells divide to make muscle cells, bone or skin cells make new bone or skin cells. But the great Idea worked out so that certain cells were special. These could grow and split in two to form *all* the parts of a *whole new growing creature*.

These are called *germ* cells. "Germ" doesn't mean only something that causes sickness and disease. It comes from a Latin word meaning the beginnings or *buds* from which things sprout. The "germ of an idea" is that first, quick flash you get from which you build a whole plan. Germ cells are found in both plants and animals.

The female germ cell, from the mother, is the egg or *ovum*. In such an animal as a dog, cat, or human being it is as tiny as the smallest dot you can make with a pointed pencil. Frog eggs are larger and, like fish eggs, each is in a little jelly-like ball. Shark and some bird eggs are largest of all. Bird and reptile eggs are inside a tough egg shell. Fish and frog, reptile and bird eggs usually develop outside the mother; such animals as kittens, puppies and human children develop inside her. But no matter how small the ovum, the *sperm* cell from the father is much tinier. The sperm swims to the ovum and joins with it. This is called *fertilizing* the ovum.

The sperm does two things when its nucleus unites with the nucleus of the ovum. First, it starts the ovum on its way to dividing into new cells—it sets it in action, or activates it. Second, it carries certain traits from the father into the ovum, which already bears certain traits from the mother. These traits determine many things

12

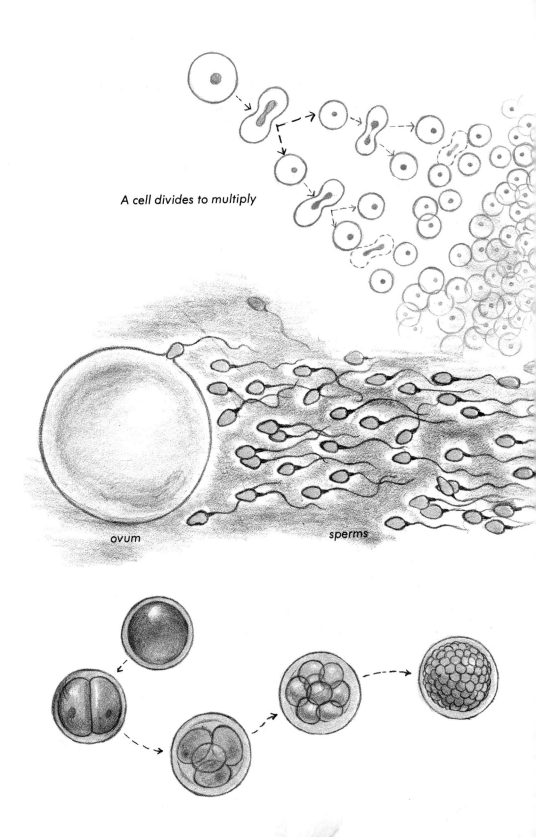

A cell divides to multiply

ovum

sperms

about the creature-to-be. A little turtle may have markings more like its father than its mother. Three kittens of a litter may be black like their mother, the fourth may be gray and white, resembling its father.

People used to believe that a whole new little creature was already formed inside its parent, waiting only to grow bigger and be born, and inside it was another one, like boxes one inside another. We know now that isn't true. But it is a marvel beyond words the way the tiny egg, whether that of fish or bird, snake or monkey, can grow and divide, grow and divide, many millions of times. In the case of a human being the first cell, in just a few months' time, increases a billion times in weight to turn into a squalling newborn baby.

There are many other facts to think long and hard about. How can the sperm and egg, tiny even under a microscope, made mostly of water themselves, carry chemicals within that cause the covering cells of the new creature to turn into scales or skin, feathers or fur—that keep a baby alligator, in other words, from hatching with feathers instead of scales, or fish fry from having fur instead of scales? What makes one part of an egg become eye, another fin— or hoof, wing or paw—always on the right animal? A fertilized human egg, with little structure which can be seen except through a strong microscope, may someday produce a boy or girl with a smile nearly like its mother's, or perhaps more like its father's, a little like its ancestors', and still all its own, through the mystery of heredity and growth. How do chemicals get a smile into the wee-est of eggs? Scientists can tell us some of the answers—but the wonder of how it all happens leaves us spellbound.

That unseen, dark time after an egg is fertilized and before a baby creature is born—snakelet, insect or fish; pollywog, bird or turtle; puppy, monkey or human child—moves step by step through many mysteries. The unborn or unhatched animal is called an *embryo* (EM-bree-o). Let's take some glimpses inside some eggs and see what happens to some embryos.

14

3. Eggs of the Waters

In the waters, in the "cradle of the deep," life on Earth probably began. The seas—lakes and rivers, too—are full of many kinds of living things that spawn huge numbers of eggs. Vast quantities of eggs of many kinds drift in the *plankton,* the nearly-microscopic life, plant as well as animal, that drifts through the oceans' waters, and which larger sea creatures live on. Fish often produce eggs, sometimes called roe, in enormous numbers—the cod may lay up to nine million a year! Fish eggs are often quite transparent, and this crystal clearness protects them from being seen. Those eggs which float usually contain a drop or two of silvery, gleaming oil inside to buoy them up, like life preservers. The fry, or newly hatched fish, look like slivers of glass.

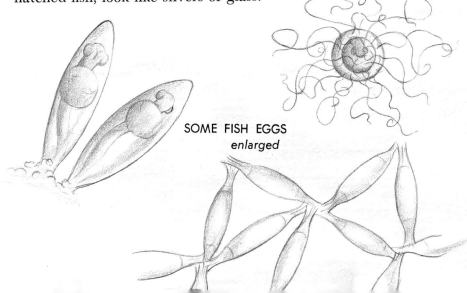

SOME FISH EGGS
enlarged

Many fish eggs, especially fresh-water ones, sink. This prevents their being washed downstream by river currents. Such kinds are usually sticky, and some pick up sand grains that weight them down as they swell up with water right after being laid. Some others have thread-like streamers to anchor them. The half-invisible fry are delicate and feeble, but gain strength and speed—if they escape being eaten.

Do you remember how heavy you feel after coming out of the lake or swimming pool or ocean? Life in water is much easier than life on dry land in many ways, and there is no reason why living things should leave it, unless the conditions of water-living become difficult. Most of the Earth was once water; only a small fraction was land. All the life that existed was in the waters. Yet the land was *there,* and sooner or later something had to set foot, or fin, on it.

Some early fishes, somewhere, millions of years ago, learned to drag themselves from some drying-up pond to a puddle a little distance away, gasping in the harsh air. Millions of years later land life had improved to the point where it could live ashore much more easily and get around more quickly.

If someone discovered a dinosaur still alive somewhere the world would be dazed with amazement, yet an animal that reveals many things about the past lives right under our noses. The frog or toad's life retells the story of the fish that came to land, not exactly as it happened, but something very much like it. The life histories of untold numbers of animals from past times are shrunk into some happenings in the life of one frog or toad.

For a tadpole or "pollywog" is really, in a way, just a fish—but a fish with a difference! All in a few summer weeks it turns into another kind of animal as if touched by magic, and becomes a young frog or toad that can live on land. But when it is an adult it absolutely must return to the water, or to wet places, to lay eggs that will hatch into fish-like water creatures.

16

Let's take a closer look at a frog egg as it develops. Eggs of our most common frogs and toads, and salamanders too, are laid in masses or strings in ponds, often intertwined among water plants. The father frog fertilizes the eggs as they leave the mother, and the clear, jelly-like ball around each egg swells greatly in the water. Some frogs may lay several thousand eggs at a time, though many may not survive for long. A frog's egg is very large, for an egg, and easily studied.

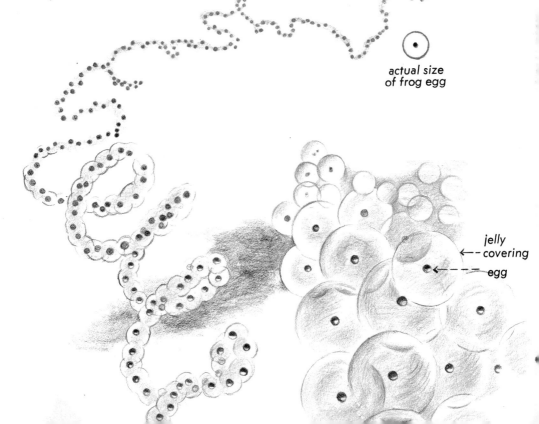

actual size
of frog egg

jelly
←-- covering
egg

The newly-laid frog egg can be seen to be dark on the top half with a light-colored lower half. If turned upside down it will slowly rotate right side up again. If held upside down for a while in an experiment it will not develop normally and will soon die. This one cell divides to become two cells, the two become four, the four eight and so on—all without the egg becoming any bigger—until a hollow ball is formed.

And now an even more spectacular happening begins. Without a microscope you can watch the lower, light half shrink away to a dot. A circle—*not* a hole—first appears in the lower half. Toward this circle all the cells start to move. They glide toward it and into the inside of the hollow ball, or *gastrula*, to take their places, each to its proper position. More than half the ball's surface ends up inside. For a while it looks as if the whole surface of the little gastrula is flowing as the cells pour down the sides; a royal procession of cells, each little grouping waiting as if for its own signal to join in.

Then the flowing comes to a stop. The one-celled egg has turned into a many-celled ball of three layers, in a basic plan found throughout nearly the entire animal kingdom.

Layer no. 1 will become the skin, brain and nervous system.

Layer no. 2 will become the muscles, heart and bones.

Layer no. 3 will line the lungs and digestive tube (mouth, stomach, intestines).

Try to picture this. Each spot on the gastrula, as the movement began, has moved to a certain other place—not just to any place—either inside or outside of the gastrula. This ball shape looks nothing like a tadpole, yet the future of each group of cells is all "mapped out" for it. A certain spot on the surface will become an eye, another spot a gill, still another the tail. They do not start out on the gastrula very near where they will end up always. (See p. 57 for a "map" of the gastrula.)

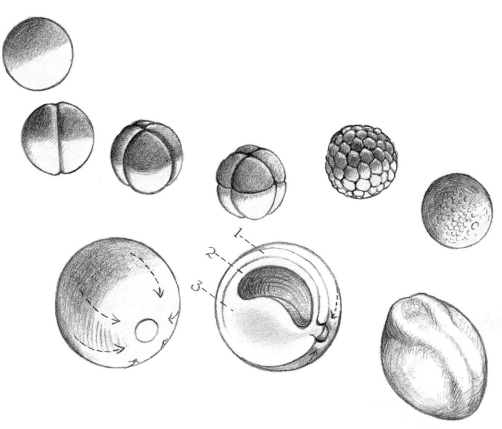

But not much longer does the ball remain a ball. It starts to lengthen out slightly as its two earliest systems begin to develop. First, the top thickens and a tube forms in it. This tube will thicken more here, thin out there, form new types of cells, send out filaments, until it has become the highly complicated brain, spinal cord and nerves. Second, another hollow tube lengthens out from front to back beneath the first one to form the digestive tube. Now it is a "tailbud embryo."

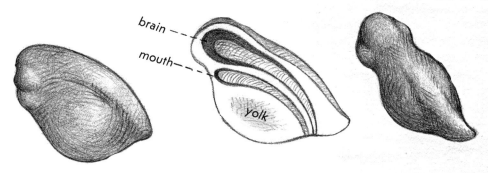

From this point on, other organs begin to form, one after another, beginning as tiny buds and pouches. Each seems to await its proper time as if its name had been called: heart, eyes, liver, muscles, ears.

A very important device is built right into the underside of the tailbud embryo. This is the yolk that came from the light-colored cells of the beginning egg, and it is present inside the digestive tube as food for the embryo to grow on. Tadpoles and fish fry still have some of this even after they have hatched, which they carry around with them like a picnic lunch until it is used up. A baby

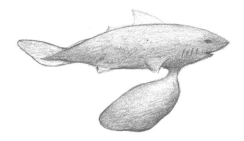

dogfish shark has a peculiar one suspended beneath him. In the yolk of these fry there is often a drop of light oil to buoy them up, just as in the eggs. But the little salmon has such a heavy yolk weighing it down that these newly hatched "alevins" must huddle under stones or in cracks until theirs is gone. They are by then a little bigger and stronger and can hunt their own dinners.

If it is warm and sunny the frog eggs develop faster than in a chill spring with frigid nights and cloudy days. The tailbud embryo is covered with fine, hair-like bristles which help him rotate within his egg. He can even twitch his stubby tail once in a while. The egg becomes softer in the water, and the little tadpole wriggles out after usually a little less than a week since his egg left the mother. He has no mouth yet; he hasn't even any workable eyes.

20

He spends his first couple of days swimming every few seconds and resting, swimming and resting. His two suckers behind where his mouth will be glue him for short periods to water plants and stones.

An opening soon breaks through beneath the snout to join the digestive tube. Now he has a mouth to eat with, for his yolk is all used up. This new mouth with its horny rim can scrape tiny plant life off slimy stones and water leaves.

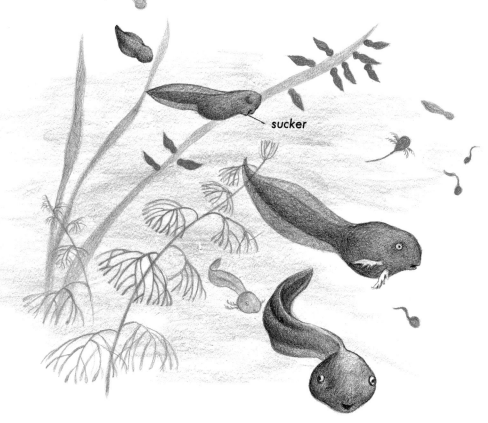

sucker

In time the miracle of change will come over him and our polly-wog will sprout back legs. When they are just about as long as his pudgy body, front legs will begin to grow. The tiny mouth of a creature that has lived only on plant life within a few days' time will turn into the great, gaping maw of an animal that lives on meat. It loses its gills, and its lungs grow so that it can breathe in air rather than take its oxygen out of the water. A frog cannot turn its neck, and so its eyes must do extra work, and they become the gigantic orbs that can be drawn back into the head bones, or skull. They also switch from being eyes that see best under water to eyes which have better vision on land.

Many other changes transform him, inside and out. His skeleton changes. His digestive tube changes, for he now lives on an entirely different kind of food. One of the most noticeable changes makes us ask: where does the tail go? It actually becomes absorbed into him. Sometimes you can see small froglets or toadlets hopping about, still with a shriveling little flap of tail wagging behind them.

But for now, the little tadpole in the water eats, eats, eats. It becomes skillful and quick in its movements. It is on its way. The way will be hard, and its chances of being eaten are greater than its chances of surviving. Perhaps only one or two of all the brothers and sisters in the egg-mass at last will grow up to make their way back from the land to the water when spring calls them.

Frogs, toads and salamanders are all called *amphibians* (from two Greek words meaning "on both sides" and "life"), because they are creatures of two worlds, water and air. True, they are bound to wet places, but not all amphibians must lay their eggs in actual water. Some salamanders lay theirs in moist, rotting logs in shady woods, or beneath damp leaves. Some hang them from wet cave walls, others in thick moss near ponds.

You may be lucky enough to find fish or frog eggs in river, pond, lake or stream. If you search for salamanders or their eggs in the woods, be sure to turn back stones, logs or leaves the way you

found them—they make better homes, or possible homes, for many forms of life that way. Take only a few of the eggs you find and try to raise them under conditions as nearly natural as possible.

4. The Egg Comes to Land

Except for so many of them being eaten, eggs in many ways had an easy time of it in the water. Most important, they were kept from drying out. Second, the temperature of the water changed little during the time they were developing. Third, the water itself was a perfect cradle where a fragile little egg could be protected and rocked in the sea's gentle motion. In comparison to all this, how harsh life on land would be!

For where on Earth could a tasty, tender little egg be hidden from hungry, searching eyes and still find warmth? How, if it found warmth, could it avoid being cooked in the sun's heat? How could its delicate inmate be protected from drying out? And how could the little embryo inside have all its needs met—growing, getting nourishment and oxygen, giving off wastes?

All these problems changed with the slow development of the very remarkable "new egg." The egg got a shell and became "boxed off" in a private world of its own. At the same time a system of bags inside the shell came into being. The bags are called *sacs*. There are four altogether. With the aid of these sacs the little animal inside could be longer in developing than could fish or tadpole, and thus be better prepared to face the world, and the more likely it would be to survive. The more young that survived, the fewer eggs needed by which each animal kind would live on, and the more complicated could become an egg in the mother. The fewer she produced, the better care she could take of what she had. And the better their chances would become. A mother robin or turtle wouldn't need to lay nine million eggs!

Reptile and bird eggs are much alike, but reptile eggs are harder to obtain for study than are a certain barnyard bird's. A chicken egg is a good example of the egg of any bird. If you carefully break open a hen's familiar egg into a saucer, you can examine it. Wait until it is still and then observe it as you have never done before. This one most likely came from a large poultry farm where eggs are less likely to be fertilized. If it has been, the tiny beginning embryo is dead, as the egg has not been *incubated*, or kept in a place of the proper warmth (102° F.). But you are looking at a very remarkable object—a single cell. Germ cells are very large cells, and the bird's egg is the largest of all cells. This is mostly because of its tremendous quantity of yolk or "yellow." A filmy tissue surrounds the yolk, as you can see.

26

Only the yolk is the cell itself—the "egg white" or albumen is not properly part of the cell. The egg with the yolk rotates as it comes down the egg canal. As it turns round and round, the albumen is added in layers, and is twisted at its front and back ends. The shell is added last; its calcium and other minerals are put out by glands of the egg canal. There is a little air space in one end.

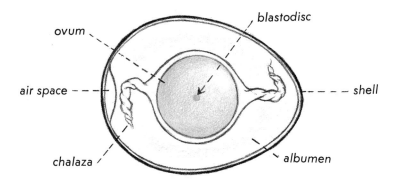

On top of the yolk you will see a small, almost invisible circle. In this spot, and this alone, the chick will develop in a fertilized egg. This little disc is called the *blastodisc*. It begins by dividing into cells—two, four, eight, sixteen and so on. And then a small groove appears in the many-celled blastodisc.

Cells in the beginning animal body have very strange abilities. One of these is the ability to *migrate* as they divide. They seem to flow into place; to leave one place and set out for another as their numbers increase. In the frog's ball-shaped gastrula the cells flowed down the sides and some of them into the hollow inside to form three layers. In the chick blastodisc, cells migrate toward the groove to flow into place beneath it, forming three layers in the blastodisc. From these three layers come the same systems and organs as in the frog (see p. 18).

We spoke of the marvelous invention of the egg, with its bags, or sacs, inside the shell. These have not yet begun to form, but are about to. If a bird is to survive it must have them. There must be a sac, first, to hold the embryo—a sac filled with fluid for the developing chick to float in; its own private pond. In this it will not only be protected from drying out, but it can exercise its feeble muscles, just as you can lift a heavy stone in water you could never lift on land. There must also be a sac to hold the yolk the chick will need to grow on. Its yolk will not be built right into its body as was the food supply of the tad or fish fry, for the land creature —reptile or bird—needs more yolk to carry it farther. Highly important is the sac into which go the waste products from the growing animal's body—a sort of small, disposable bathroom. This sac, the yolk sac, and the embryo's sac of fluid are all surrounded by a fourth sac just inside the shell.

But you may well wonder how, as the heart and other organs begin, a flat little disc can grow legs under it for a round little chicken to run around on.

28

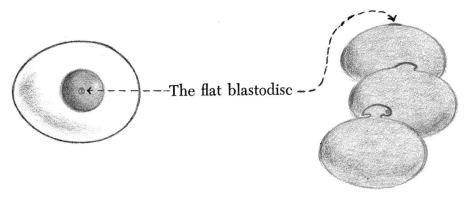

The flat blastodisc

grows up off the yolk at its front and back ends, while its outside covering pinches in underneath. This is how the embryo becomes separated from the yolk.

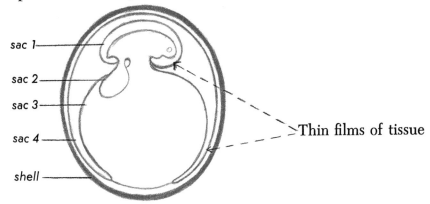

sac 1

sac 2

sac 3

sac 4

shell

Thin films of tissue

grow out from beneath the embryo to form the four sacs. Finally, the second sac, the "disposable bathroom," grows out to join with the fourth and these surround chick and yolk entirely. The yolk and waste sacs connect to the chicken beneath the belly while it is in the egg.

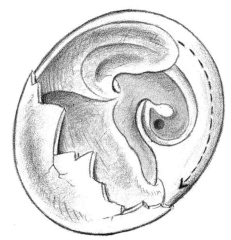

The layer right underneath the shell will become covered by a network of blood vessels. These take oxygen from the air and return used gases to the air through the shell, which has very tiny pores through it. If a bird egg is held under water a short time the embryo inside will die. If a fertilized egg is kept in an incubator to develop, a dish of water should be kept there too, to keep the air moist, or the chick inside may die. Some desert birds wet their feathers to bring moisture to their clutch of eggs.

Now the chick is safe inside its own, complete world. The sac that the embryo floats in actually contains a kind of muscle cell which rocks the chick gently in its own private ocean! The mother hen, or other bird parents taking turns on their nests, must keep the eggs warm by sitting on them. This is called brooding. (Parent birds in hot climates must cool their eggs off at times!) The mother turns the eggs over now and then so that they will develop properly. Meanwhile the parts of the embryo are growing in their certain manner and order. The brain, which is at first most of the chicken, puts out eyes and ears. Nerves come out of the brain and spinal cord, later to connect up with other parts, especially wings and legs. The "wing-buds" and "leg-buds" begin to grow. As early as the third day after the egg has been fertilized the little cluster of cells that will become the heart will begin to move. They will twitch at first, then they will pulsate—slowly for a while, but soon the heart is beating its first, uneven beats. It has nothing to pump at first, for the blood vessels themselves must take form, connect up with each other and the heart, and the forming blood must begin to flow within them. Inside the dark egg, unseen and un-heard, life has begun to march.

After nearly three weeks in the egg the little chick is a bit cramped. It has been resting comfortably on its soft mattress of yolk, which through the days and nights has shrunk to pillow-size. The egg-white has gone into furnishing the water for the chick's needs. But by the time the chick's twenty-one days in the egg are

30

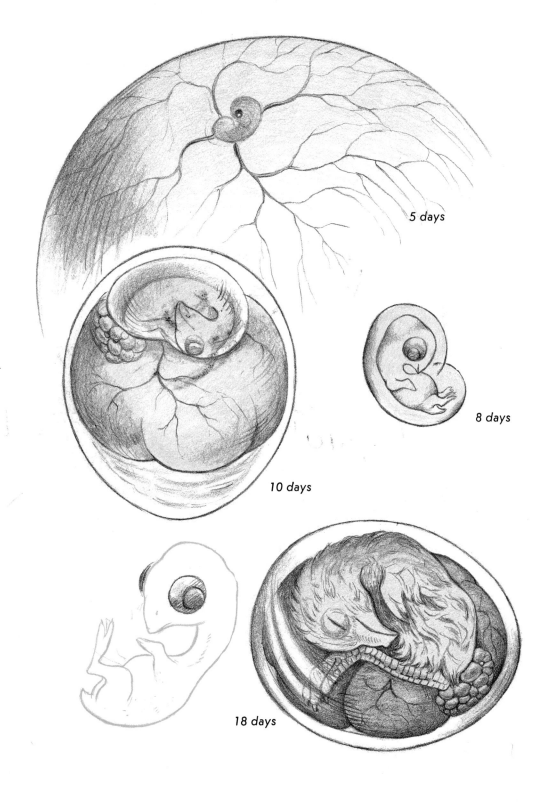

5 days

8 days

10 days

18 days

nearly up, the outer sac has taken much of the calcium out of the shell and it has been absorbed into the chick's bones—the bones become stronger, the eggshell weaker. The sacs are little more than tight films stretched around the chicken now. The embryo has used up nearly all its yolk and has grown to fit snugly into its tight quarters. And on its beak is a little bump, the "egg tooth" (or shell tooth). Somehow the chick feels that its safe, private world is no longer big enough for it—it wants out! And the egg tooth is just in the right position to start protesting. The chick has a special muscle in the back of its neck also to give extra strength for pecking at the shell. For hours it chips around its prison, squirming and shoving as much as it can with legs and head. Sometimes a muffled "peep" can be heard from inside the egg as the chick struggles for breath.

Wet and unsteady, it finally staggers out on awkward legs. At hatching time important changes have also taken place inside it so that heart, lungs and blood flow can adjust to the demands of an active life.

Bird eggs are often quite beautiful in color, and often speckled or mottled. This coloring may serve to protect them in making them look more like the sun and shadows and to blend in with their surroundings. They should never be touched or taken if you discover any.

The first animals to be able to live outside the water were the ambitious amphibians, the group that became our frogs, toads and salamanders. We know how they grew lungs so that they could breathe in air, but each year, usually in spring, they return to wet places to lay eggs. The new light and warmth call them; the urges within their own bodies send them back to their ponds.

But the reptiles go a step beyond the amphibians. Turtles, crocodiles, snakes and lizards—all reptiles—are land creatures. They all have the "new type" of egg with sacs, that can survive very well on land (although some reptile mothers retain the eggs inside them

SOME REPTILE EGGS

until the young are born). True, many reptiles do spend much of their time in the water—crocodiles and alligators, water snakes, some turtles—but that is because they have become used to it. They come ashore to lay their eggs, while the amphibians go back to the water to lay theirs!

Although most reptile mothers are far from being the best mothers in the world, their eggs are better provided for than those of most fish. A crude nesting place, hidden under stones, in burrows or under leaves is often nestled into by snakes. Turtle mothers dig holes in the ground or sand, deposit their eggs, cover them up and forget about them. Turtle eggs—all reptile eggs, for that matter— are white, or nearly so, never colored or speckled. They do not need to be, as buried eggs need no protective disguise to conceal them from hungry eyes. These eggs cannot dry out too much in the ground, and some turtles moisten their eggs before leaving them.

A few snakes brood their young, and many snake mothers guard and defend their clutch of eggs from harm. But the snakelets get no care at all. Yet, like lizard babies, they hatch quite able to look after themselves, and quickly scurry around to begin. Snakelets, like baby turtles, have an egg tooth for slitting their eggs. Some snakes are born already hatched (turtles and lizards rarely) as the mother keeps the eggs inside her where the babies hatch out. Some are born having had no shell surrounding them at all while in the mother. But even these babies are born with an egg tooth!

And what of the fearsome crocodile or alligator? The clumsy mother 'gator or croco surprises us by building a great nest, often spending several days thrashing about to smooth a place in the brush and tall grass, carrying in mud and water plants to construct a rather skillful nest, which she defends fiercely. She even helps her babies escape into the tall grass when they hatch.

Reptile eggs are not always "egg-shaped." A few are long, and turtle eggs are often round as ping-pong balls. Some even bounce! They are often tough and leathery and sometimes flexible. Reptile

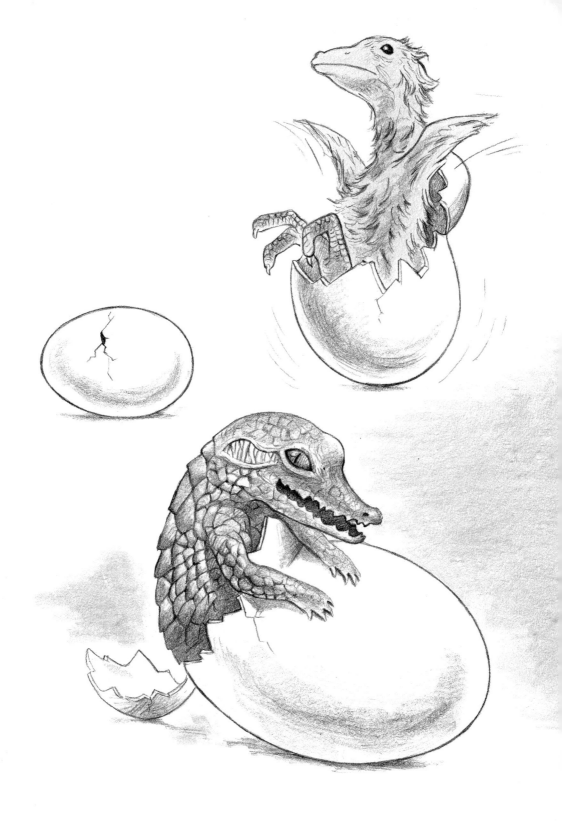

eggs often change shape as they grow. This is because they absorb water and swell.

Bird mothers and very often fathers make the best of parents, to which reptile parents can never compare. Mother birds of many kinds, and often the father too, develop a "brood patch," losing their underside feathers in order to incubate the eggs better against their warm flesh. Ducks and geese pull out feathers from underneath them in order to make a brood patch.

Turtle, snake or lizard eggs (crocodiles' eggs too, if you happen to run across any) can be examined but should be left where they are found. Reptiles as well as most other animals have enemies enough without their greatest threat—man.

SOME BIRD EGGS

crow

murre

sparrow

bluejay

pigeon

owl

night hawk

robin

hummingbird

5. Eggs Without Shells

You didn't hatch out of an egg. Neither did any cub nor kitten, colt, or kangaroo. That is because you and all those animals happen to be mammals. Mammals are animals which grow inside the mother for some time. These are born and not hatched from eggs, and are nursed with milk from the mother. But perhaps they—and you—were not so different from toads, lizards and bluebirds as you might think, for there may be some experiences in your dim pasts which were startlingly alike.

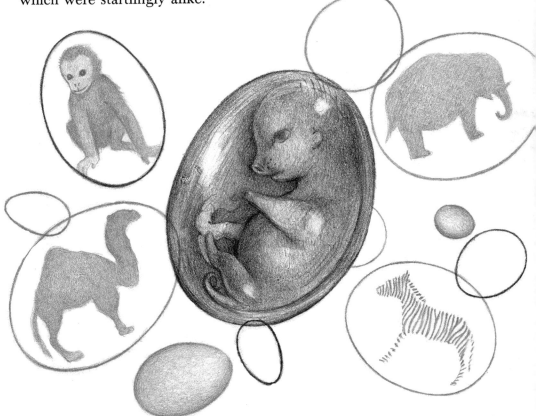

Let's go back to the waters for a moment again. Fish and most other creatures that live in the sea stand such a great risk of being devoured at one time or another, or of meeting other fates, that the mother must lay huge numbers of eggs—thousands or even millions—so that a few will survive. For this reason she cannot keep them inside her very long to develop. There are too many.

The better an invention the egg could become, with more yolk, the longer and safer an embryo could stay in it to develop. And the better it would usually be able to look after itself when it got out. The reptiles do not lay nearly as many eggs as fish and frogs do. Birds do not lay as many as reptiles do, because the mother and father bird can give such fine care to the eggs they do lay.

Some kinds of eggs even stay in the mother until they hatch inside her, and the youngsters come out. A few fish do this, some frogs, and quite a few reptiles. The word for this is *ovoviviparous* (*ovo* = egg, *vivi* = alive, *parous* = bringing forth).

Why aren't mammals hatched out of eggs? Why don't sheep, rabbits or people lay eggs and be done with it, rather than having the mother go to all the trouble of carrying her baby inside her for so long? One answer is that the offspring can be far better protected within the mother than it ever could be in an egg. Another reason is that it can have a longer time to develop, and more advanced kinds of life can then be produced. It would take a ridiculously big egg to have enough yolk stored up in it to nourish a puppy or calf—or elephant—during its development from one cell to billions. And so nature provided a way for the mammal baby to get the best care of any animal we have yet studied. It took a long time, hundreds of centuries in fact, for this method to be worked out, because it has even gone farther than the inventions of the sacs in the "new egg."

Two animals, however, were real puzzlers when first discovered. They looked like some kind of joke to people who first saw them, for they seemed to be—and are—part mammal, part reptile. The

actual size of Platypus egg

first is the Duck-billed Platypus, the second is the Spiny Anteater, or Echidna.

The first puzzler, found only in Australia, has the furry body of a mammal, the tail of a beaver, webbed feet, and a most extraordinary duck-like bill which looks as if it had been stuck on by mis-

actual size

of Echidna baby and egg

take. Furthermore, this animal actually lays eggs and supplies its young with milk, which they lap up from its furry underside!

The second animal, found only in Australia, Tasmania and nearby New Guinea, is quite as impossible. It has spines rather like a porcupine's, and its head isn't much more than a hose-like snout, which it uses to dig out and devour ants and termites. Its feet look like they were on backwards, but are powerful and clawed. It can go without food for long periods of time, as a reptile can; several weeks when necessary. And it, too, lays eggs out of which its babies hatch.

Scientists studied these two and found that they bore many internal features of reptiles as well as those of mammals. The Duck-billed Platypus lays from one to three, usually two, eggs in a damp nest of leaves at the far end of a long tunnel dug in the bank of a stream. The young have an egg tooth when they hatch! The Spiny Anteater lives in drier places than the streams of the Platypus, but both these two strangest of animals, these reptile-like mammals, are In-Betweens which give the best care to their babies of any offspring that hatch from eggs.

But certainly the most fascinating of animal babies may be a kind that can scarcely be called babies at all—they are little more than embryos when they are born. You know their mother. She has a pouch—a furry pocket underneath her into which her offspring go when they are born, and where they are nursed.

The opossum, or possum, gives birth to her babies when they are still the most helpless and half-formed of living beings. She has from eight or nine to as many as twenty-four at a time, and they are so tiny that an entire litter of eighteen or twenty will fit in a teaspoon! But their front paws are remarkably well developed. With these "hands" they pull themselves the two or three inches to her pouch, where they stay to be nursed and grow until they are around three months old. At this time they venture out for some short peeks at the world.

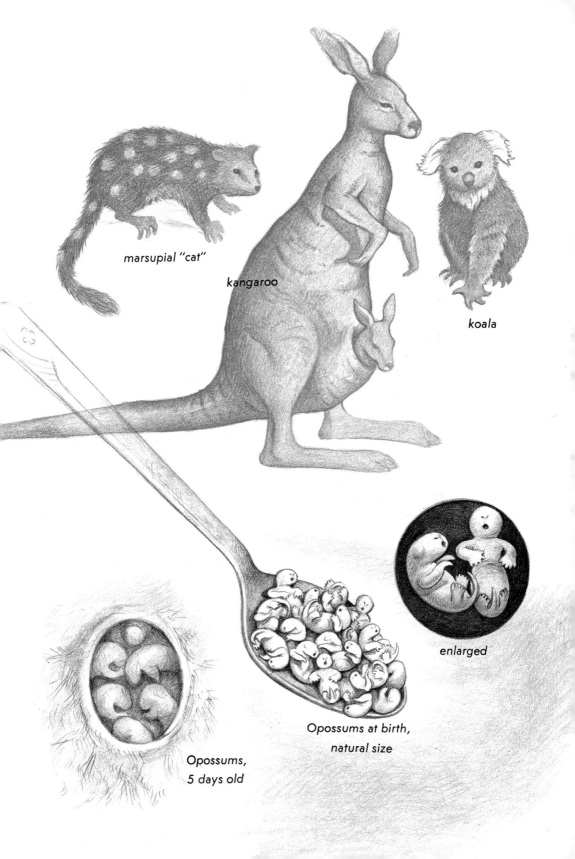

marsupial "cat"

kangaroo

koala

Opossums at birth,
natural size

enlarged

Opossums,
5 days old

A possum is called a *marsupial* because the proper name for its pouch is a *marsupium*. There are other marsupials in the world, though our possum is found only in North America. There are other kinds of possums in South America, and Australia, on the other side of the world, has some most peculiar pouched mammals. There are little "mouse opossums," and the Australian native cat, wolf, rat and mole. These are not related to true cats, wolves, rats or moles but merely resemble these animals a bit and have pouches for the care of their young. Better known is the "teddy bear" koala, but this cub-like animal was once trapped in too great numbers for its fur, and there are scarcely any left to see. Best known of all are the kangaroos. But we don't have to go to Australia to gaze on strange marsupials. We have one of the strangest of all almost in our own backyard—the possum.

The egg-laying mammals and the marsupials are a very small part of the great group of mammals, the commonest animals we see around us daily. What differences there are among members of this group—from the mouse to the elephant, from aardvark to zebra!

But all of them before birth go through the same necessary stages. The mouse embryo goes through the *same basic steps* as the elephant embryo. In fact, all many-celled animal life follows the same basic pattern. One egg becomes two-celled, two cells become four, four become eight. The cells divide to multiply! The embryo grows through a pattern of early cells which look all alike, but they put out new cells different from the cells they come from, and so bone, muscle and skin are formed at the right time, in the right place.

If you could compare early embryos of probably any kind, you would note the surprising fact that even an expert might not be able to tell them apart, except for size. A pig that has developed a short time looks almost exactly like the early stage of a dog, a human being, a monkey. In fact, these even look remarkably like an

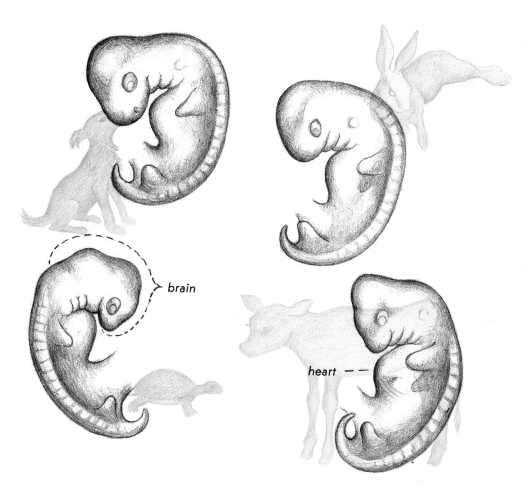

brain

heart —

SOME EARLY EMBRYOS

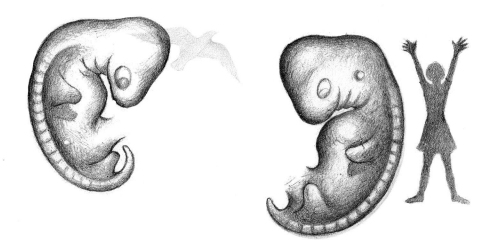

embryonic chicken or turtle. The earlier the stage, the more alike all mammals look. We are closer to other animals than we think. The farther we go in our development, the more different become our ways from theirs. We would like to think that our behavior becomes superior, too.

The embryo's home inside the mother is not so different from the inside of an egg. It only lacks the shell. But the mother has a special organ in which to protect her growing young one. It is the womb, or uterus (YOO-ter-us), which is made of thick muscle. All the sacs found in the bird's egg are in some way inside the uterus. Of course the sac of fluid (the *amniotic* sac) must be there for the embryo to float in, to be kept moist and protected from bumps and blows. Next is the sac carrying waste from the embryo. The yolk sac, too, is represented, but there is no yolk after the first few days, as the embryo no longer needs to get its nourishment from stored food. The outer sac forms many tiny blood vessels which draw nourishment from the mother's blood supply and carry it to the baby. Where this sac joins the uterus a new organ is formed, the size of a thick saucer, and this is connected to the baby's *umbilicus* ("navel") by blood vessels which wind through a long, white cord. The saucer-shaped organ is called the "after-birth" (placenta) because it comes out right after the baby is born. The animal mother usually cuts the cord with her teeth when her young one is born, and it seals itself off with a kind of jelly that forms inside it.

And so all mammal embryos, including the forming human baby, go through the same orderly processes, step by step, well protected and well nourished, for the time needed to make a perfect member of its kind. How long is needed to make each one? Here are some times that different embryos require in the uterus from the time the egg is fertilized until they are born.

opossum	12-13 days
mouse	3 weeks
rabbit	34 days

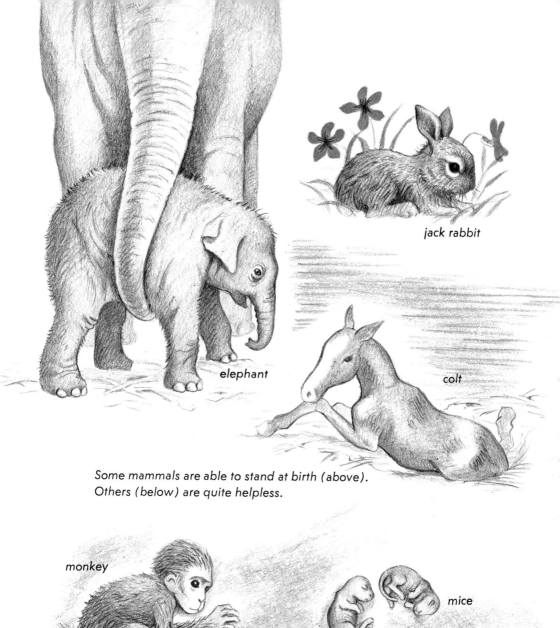

jack rabbit

elephant

colt

Some mammals are able to stand at birth (above).
Others (below) are quite helpless.

monkey

mice

puppy

hedgehog

dog	a little over 2 months
cat	a little over 2 months
tiger	3½ months
chimpanzee	about 9 months (270 days)
cow	about 9 months
human being	about 9 months
whale	11 months
horse	11½ months
camel	14 months
elephant	just under 2 years

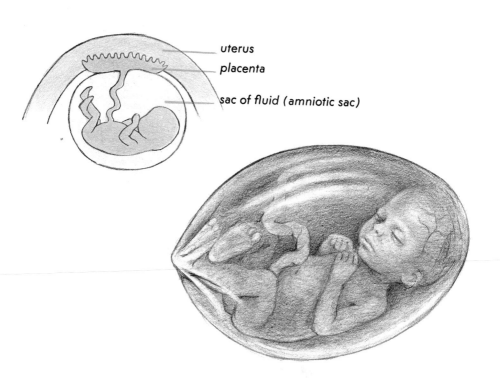

uterus

placenta

sac of fluid (amniotic sac)

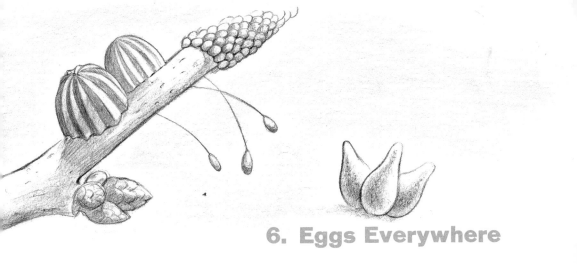

6. Eggs Everywhere

Well, eggs aren't exactly everywhere, but you can find them hiding a lot closer than you would think. Insects, as always, hold many surprises, and some of their eggs come in astonishing shapes. Insect mothers often provide for their young by laying eggs where they will find a food supply waiting for them when they hatch, depending on what they eat. Their eggs are laid on twigs, on leaves and under them, in bark, wood and on living caterpillars. Some grasshoppers lay eggs in the ground; many beetles deposit eggs in old logs. The mayfly or dragonfly you watch skimming low over a pond or lake, even dipping its tail-end in sometimes, may be laying its eggs on or just beneath the water's surface.

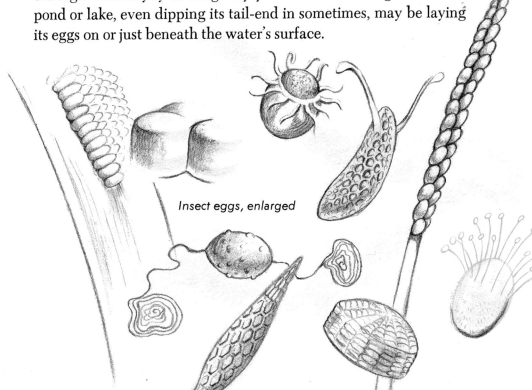

Insect eggs, enlarged

You can find ant eggs under stones in park or garden, and watch the nursemaid ants whip them out of sight down dark passageways when disturbed by the light of day. Some mosquitoes make floating rafts of their eggs on ponds. Big, swollen balls on twigs of bushes or on plant stems, or even on leaves, may be *galls* in which eggs will hatch, and the young will eat the plant's juices before escaping from their nursery. Bubbly, sudsy nests are found on flower and weed stems in the woods and fields—this froth protects new-hatched youngsters from weather and from hungry eyes.

Insect eggs and embryos have the same basic needs as do all other eggs and embryos. The delicate, growing creature needs to be guarded from bumps, weather and from being eaten. Some eggs have tough, strong shells; others in protected situations have a thin, tissue-like covering. The embryo is in its fluid bath inside, and has a good amount of yolk as the stored food it needs to grow on.

Some insect eggs are waterproofed with a waxy surface. Some, laid in plant stems, have tiny tubes that draw plant sap into the egg as its water supply. A grasshopper egg has a certain spot on it through which it takes moisture. Insect eggs must also "breathe," taking in oxygen through their shells and giving off waste gases.

Have you wondered how the sperm can get through the insect eggshell to fertilize the ovum? It enters through a tiny hole in one end. But the sperm enters the bird egg before the shell has been added. In either case, the sperm nucleus joins the ovum nucleus to begin the multiplying of cells as the egg grows. Some insects can actually lay eggs that are not fertilized but still grow into embryos.

The little insect has to break out of his egg in some way. It does not have an egg tooth, but some have "hatching spines" that help split the egg. Some just bump off an "egg cap" with their heads to get free. Caterpillars simply gnaw their way out.

Before hatching, new insects swallow the fluid in their egg, which swells them up and gives them strength. A most interesting

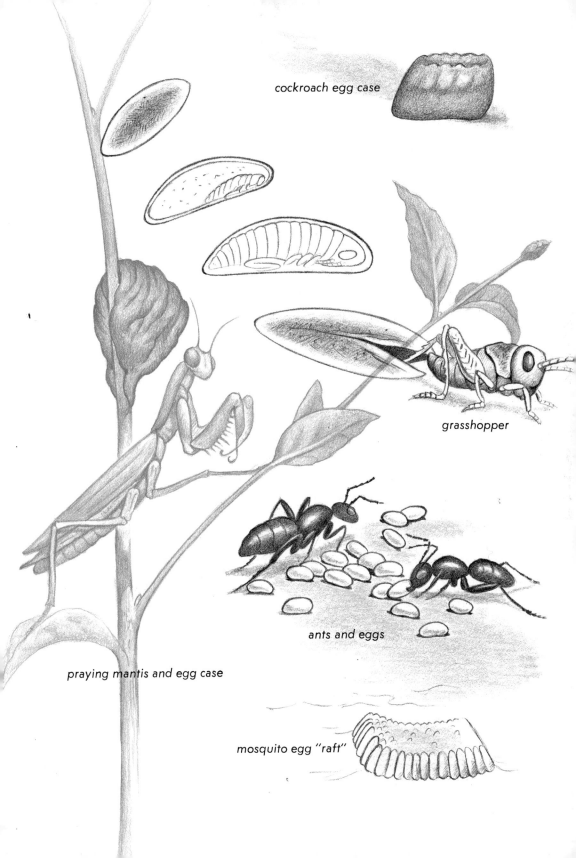

cockroach egg case

grasshopper

praying mantis and egg case

ants and eggs

mosquito egg "raft"

fact is that most insect offspring do not look a bit like their parents when they hatch. Caterpillars are an example; they go through several stages before becoming butterflies. The new-hatched insect, like the tadpole which looked nothing at all like its frog or toad parent, is called a *larva*. Grasshoppers do not hatch as a larva, however, but just as a small grasshopper. The stages that a larva goes through before becoming an adult is a whole huge subject in itself.

Great multitudes of other animal life lay eggs—little-known, usually small kinds, living out their lives rarely seen by human eyes. But their eggs carry them into the future just as they have brought them out of the distant past.

Spiders often make good mothers, after a fashion. Their eggs are nearly always wrapped in a silken blanket. Some spider eggs are tiny pearls seen through a thin network of silk threads; other eggs are protected in stiff, firm balls. Some spider mothers manage to carry their huge egg sacs, or cocoons, around with them. Fuzzy orange egg sacs the size of a small pea can be found around old logs or sheds; white disks woven in gleaming silk are common on old fences, boards and stones. Egg sacs are hung between plant stems, half-hidden by a tangled curtain of silken threads. Some kinds are wrapped in a rolled-up leaf.

Spiderlings often hatch out of eggs laid in the fall after a very short time, but remain inside the cocoon huddled up through the winter with brothers and sisters, before breaking out in the spring. Yes—the baby spider has an egg tooth too!

Many more kinds of eggs are found in the sea besides those of fish. The octopus hangs hers from cave ceilings or in stony cracks under the water. Starfish, sea urchins, barnacles, crabs, and many other undersea dwellers release untold millions of eggs. Instinct calls the mother sometimes to fight to protect her eggs; more often it is only to release them in the best spot for their survival and then depart.

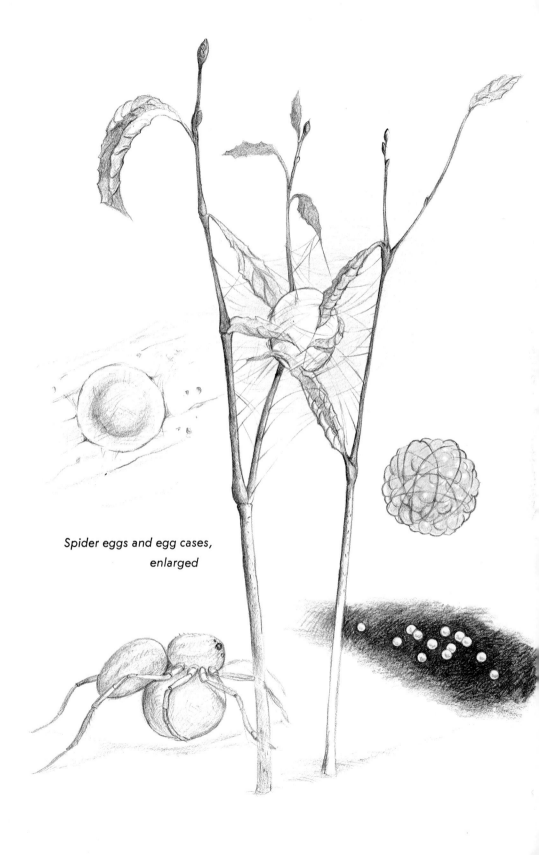

*Spider eggs and egg cases,
enlarged*

Snails of ocean, fresh water or land are plentiful for you to observe. Some snails can fertilize their eggs themselves, and you can take home a single snail and find that it may lay its clear jelly-globs, sometimes very small. You must look closely—on water stems, leaves, stones or twigs, or under seaweed tossed up on the beach. The underside of water lily leaves is an excellent place to find them. Inside the jelly-pats little white specks can be seen. These are the new-forming embryos.

Raise the fresh-water snails in a jar of water at home, preserving natural conditions as much as you can. If possible, examine a few of the specks through a microscope. You may sit up half the night marveling over the forming snails rotating in their glass jelly bubbles. When they hatch you can observe their tiny perfection with a magnifying glass as they ever so slowly crawl up the inside of the glass.

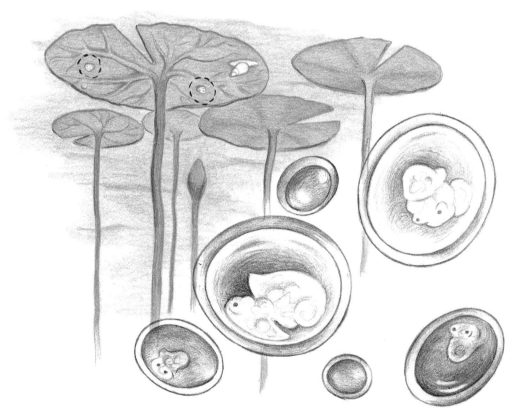

7. How Do We Know?

The tadpole grows fat and lively and many-celled. We see that it gets its back legs before its front ones. We observe that the last part of the tail may disappear much more slowly than did the first part, as we study all the changes that pass over our little tad. We learn by watching these things closely. But this isn't always enough. People—and all creatures—may act one way under normal, easy circumstances and behave quite differently under abnormal or difficult circumstances—when something goes wrong—and so we learn about them, or ourselves. We can carry out experiments on eggs and embryos by creating different or abnormal circumstances to learn what we would not find out otherwise. At this time the embryos would feel no pain.

By so doing we often ask more questions than we can answer, for each new finding creates new questions. The study of eggs and embryos is called Embryology. Let's take a glimpse into some of the work done by embryologists to gain more understanding.

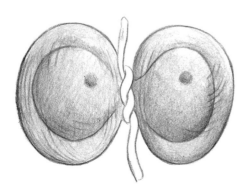

It takes some imagination to ask the proper questions. What do you think would happen to the embryo if you removed half the beginning egg, taking away one of the first two cells? What would happen if you could find a way to tie an egg through the middle? Would these eggs be killed, or, if they lived, what kind of embryo would be formed?

What do you think would happen if you cut out a part of one egg and could make that part grow onto another embryo? Perhaps this couldn't even be done. If it could, do you think it would make any difference which part of the egg you cut out to graft onto another one?

Do you think that a certain part of the early egg always grows into the same part—an eye, leg or gill—or can it grow into any part?

And what do you think it is that makes a certain part, let's say the brain, start growing at exactly the right time? What is to prevent the leg or heart from starting ahead of time, and what kind of creature might result if things grew out of order?

And the biggest question of all: what difference does it all make? Why bother to investigate such things, anyway? Is the person who knows some of the answers any better off than someone who doesn't? Does such knowledge change baseball scores, or make anyone better looking or richer?

One of the earliest experiments turned into something of an argument about splitting an egg in two. In 1888, Wilhelm Roux, the first scientist to attempt such experiments, tried to remove one cell of a two-cell egg, and the cell that remained grew into half an embryo. But four years later, Hans Driesch shook up some two-cell eggs in sea water, separating the cells from each other. Each of his half-eggs went on to form whole embryos.

What could such different results mean? Roux had used frog eggs, but Driesch had used eggs of the sea urchin (related to starfish and sand dollars), which were easier to separate cell from cell. When better methods were found to perform such delicate opera-

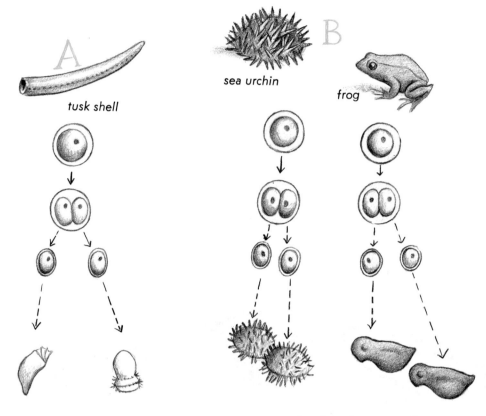

tusk shell

sea urchin

frog

Some eggs (A) will develop only halves of animals when first two cells are separated. Others (B) will go on to form whole animals.

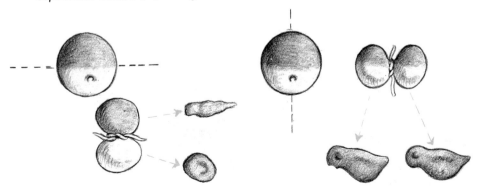

The egg must be tied down through the middle, not crosswise, to produce whole, normal tadpoles.

tions on the tiny frog egg, each half also went on to form a complete tadpole embryo.

These experiments and others, around 1900, led to another discovery—that all many-celled animal life is divided into two great groups. One needs the whole egg to develop properly. This includes earthworms, snails and clams, octopuses, and insects. The second huge group, including starfish and sea urchins and all animals with backbones (fish, reptiles, birds, human beings), can adjust itself in early stages to having part, or even half, removed. The remaining cell or cells can take over for the missing part.

Several matters of importance were proved by tying a fine hair tightly around the middle of a salamander egg, after many trials and failures. One result was that the egg would go on to form two complete salamanders joined at the tail if the hair was not tied too tightly.

Another type of experiment was begun by a German embryologist named Walther Vogt. Looking at the gastrula through a microscope he somehow performed the delicate feat of placing dots of colored stain at various points. Then as the gastrula grew and developed he could watch what happened to the marks. He must have been greatly astonished to see the little spots move across the ball, like cloud shadows might look moving across the Earth to a pilot very high up. But it was the cells themselves which were streaming down toward the little circle on the gastrula. They moved into place, some inside, some outside the hollow ball. Vogt then could make "maps" of the gastrula, telling where each little group of cells would end up in the embryo. They told what the fate of each area would be, and so were called "fate maps."

And so the beginning and end of the three layers could be traced as they flowed into place. Embryologists could tell which part would finally become brain, eyes, digestive tube, heart, gills and so on—*each at its proper time.* But how does each "know" when its proper time is?

56

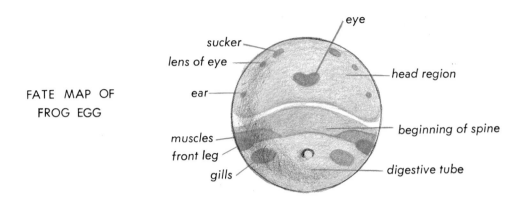

FATE MAP OF
FROG EGG

eye

sucker

lens of eye

ear

head region

beginning of spine

muscles

front leg

gills

digestive tube

"Does one part," a man named Spemann asked himself, "does one part grow all by itself into what it is to become? Or does something else *cause* it to develop into just that part?"

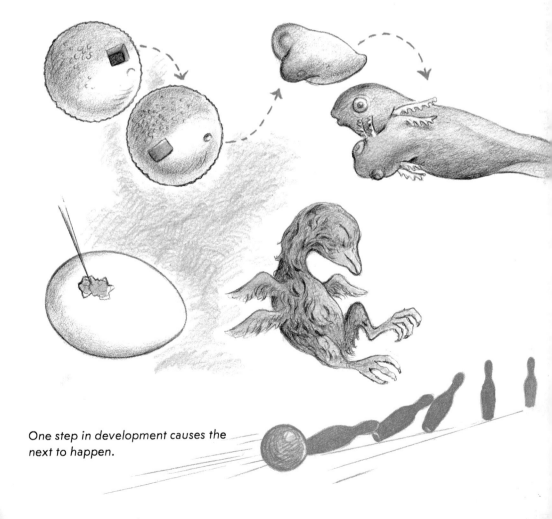

One step in development causes the next to happen.

He took a bit of tissue that a "fate map" told him would become an eye, and put it into a chemical solution. It lived and grew for a while, but became nothing in particular. "All by itself" it developed only into a mass of cells.

But when Spemann took an eye-to-be area from a tadpole gastrula and transplanted it into another part of another embryo, it grew into whatever that other region would normally become. That is, when he put it into a gill region, instead of becoming eye it developed into gill parts. Wherever it was put, it developed into whatever normally would be in that region.

But if Spemann took an eye-to-be part just a little later, from an embryo perhaps only a few hours older, it would develop into an eye no matter where it was grafted onto the embryo! By taking a very little patch of tissue at the proper time and transplanting it from one embryo to another he could even grow a second head on a salamander.

And so it was found that most parts are able to form practically anything at all at an early stage—but not later. But, reasoned the scientists, what makes a part "decide" what it will become, and when? If the embryo goes through stages, step after step, always in exactly the right order, could it be that somehow one step *causes* the next to happen? That way nothing could very easily get out of order, for each step would depend on the readiness of the step before it. The experiments began to show how each step can set off the next one in a sort of chain reaction.

Scientists next began trying to determine just what does this— is it a chemical substance, and if so, where does it come from? If it is, is it just one, or is it many different substances for the different organs and reactions? Or is it simply the touch of one cell on the next? Or is it something inside the cell, inside the nucleus even? With ever better tools to work with, men get down to ever smaller and more complicated worlds.

58

A   Animal types whose eggs will not adjust if cut in two at beginning stages, but will form half animals.

B   Animal types whose eggs will adjust if cut in two at beginning stages, and will form whole animals.

And so we come to the biggest question of all: what good is all this? Are we any better off, knowing how tadpoles and piglets spend their time before seeing the light of day?

It would take several books to answer those questions. Perhaps you can think of some answers to them yourself. One could be that, because in figuring out these puzzles, we might learn more about why some babies are not normal at birth—what goes wrong to keep them from being as perfectly made as most of us are lucky enough to be. Another is because the secrets in the growing, changing cells might let us learn more about the causes and cures of diseases—and better ways to stay healthy. We might even find ways of replacing injured or useless parts: a kidney, hand, or heart. And because, as we find out more about where man, and all life, came from we find out more about the mysteries of our relationships to all other animals. And because man was made to learn, and the understanding he gets from learning brings him greater happiness than as if he knew nothing.

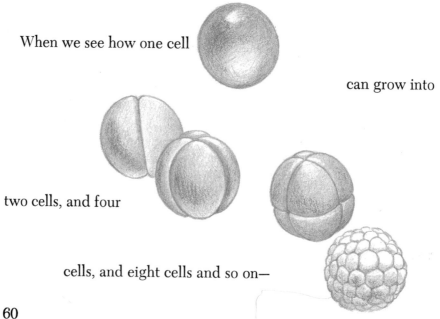

When we see how one cell

can grow into

two cells, and four

cells, and eight cells and so on—

and how each takes its place in perfect order at its proper time

until splendid creatures of countless billions of cells hop,

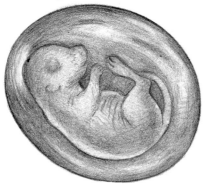

skip, swim and fly the Earth,

we are spell-
            bound with wonder.

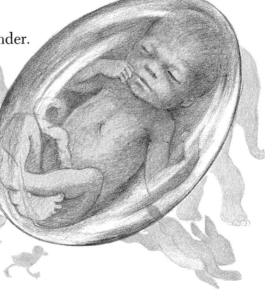

Index

The Author

Born in the small town of Sylvania, Ohio, Margaret Cosgrove became interested in botany and biology at an early age. After attending the Art Institute of Chicago and the University of Chicago, Miss Cosgrove came to New York where she spent some years as a medical illustrator, working with doctors and technicians in several large hospitals. She has broadened her interests to include all the natural sciences and has written, as well as illustrated, books in many of these fields. Much of her time has been spent working with children of all ages and backgrounds.